KING ME

ALSO BY CLINNESHA D. SIBLEY

Contraction

Hand-me-down Blues

Heels

How to Get the Mango

It Came Upon a Midnight Clear

It's in My Blood

Love Train

Lioness/Leona

Man, Damn! A Tribute to Black Wall Street

Menses

Money, Miss.

Nothin' but a Li'l Wind and Rain

Tell Martha Not to Moan

The Day It Hit

The Experiment: A Tribute to Kenneth and Mamie Clark

The Women of Strong Hope

Thorns

Tough Love

Uprooted

Very, Very Specifically

KING ME

Three One-Act Plays
Inspired by the
Life and Legacy of
Dr. Martin Luther King Jr.

CLINNESHA D. SIBLEY

The University of Arkansas Press
Fayetteville
2013

ISBN-10: 1-55728-632-9
ISBN-13: 978-1-55728-632-1

17 16 15 14 13   5 4 3 2 1

Designed by Liz Lester

⊗ The paper used in this publication meets the minimum requirements
of the American National Standard for Permanence of Paper for Printed
Library Materials Z39.48-1984.

LIBRARY OF CONGRESS CATALOGING-IN-PUBLICATION DATA

Sibley, Clinnesha D., 1984–
    [Plays. Selections]
    King me : three one-act plays inspired by the life and legacy of
Dr. Martin Luther King Jr. / Clinnesha D. Sibley.
        pages   cm
    ISBN 978-1-55728-632-1 (pbk. : alk. paper)
    1. King, Martin Luther, Jr., 1929–1968—Drama. 2. African
Americans—Drama. 3. United States—Race relations—Drama.
I. Sibley, Clinnesha D., 1984– Bound by blood. II. Sibley, Clinnesha D.,
1984– #communicate. III. Sibley, Clinnesha D., 1984– Paradox in the
parish. IV. Title.
PS3619.I243K56   2013
812'.6—dc23
                                        2012050461

To Keith.
Thank you for going on this journey with me.
I love you.

CONTENTS

PREFACE

To fully appreciate a work of dramatic literature, a reader must be willing to create strong mental images to make the story—the world of the play—come to life. By visualizing the characters in motion, in a specific time and place, a play-reading experience can be both imaginative and invigorating.

Plays are much different than other works of literature. The reader is not bogged down in narration, but ushered through the human spirit with purposeful dialogue and stage directions that communicate nonverbal means of expression such as movement, stage pictures, setting, costuming, lighting, rhythm, and sound. The action of the play requires thought, tactics, and clever maneuvers by playwrights.

The first maneuver in crafting a play is the most important. It involves voice—having power and authority over what you create. Most playwrights become the source they tap into, and so becoming a creative voice in this world should not be taken lightly.

What is voice and how do you find it?

It simply begins with what's important to you and what you value as a human being in this world.

In college, I took a class in vocal pedagogy and learned how various components interact with each other to produce a unique vocal sound. When I think of my voice as a playwright and the various ingredients that blend together and power me up to write conscious dramatic literature, I can't help but acknowledge the African American Civil Rights Movement of the 1950s and 60s as a key element. This specific time period in history and the key players who transformed American society are my foundation. When I write, I generally explore how the ideals from this time period have transitioned into the morals and ambitions of today.

After a visit to the National Civil Rights Museum (formerly known as the Lorraine Motel) several years ago, my vocal chords warmed up to Dr. Martin Luther King Jr. The most riveting part of my experience in Memphis was encountering Jacqueline Smith, a black woman who occupies an outdoor table and talks to visitors about why she boycotts the museum and why we should, too. It turns out this woman was the last holdout tenant and employee at the Lorraine and was evicted in 1988 so that the sacred ground could become a tourist attraction. I bookmarked that experience, and in 2009, *Life* magazine released photographs that captured the gruesome aftermath of Dr. King's murder. Among the photos were two images of a man named Theatrice Bailey: one shows him sweeping up King's blood from the motel balcony and another, even more eerie, scraping his blood into a jar.

I was instantly drawn to how everyday followers of Dr. King were affected the night of his assassination. I wanted to create an imaginary and foreshadowing discourse between these two real-life individuals: Jackie and Theatrice. They are wonderful representations of ordinary people in extraordinary circumstances, which, to me, is a unique approach to writing historical dramas.

Playwrights enjoy their creative liberties. As a matter of fact, it's the blending of reality with fiction that makes theatre entertaining. The truth is often bent to fit the framework of the play. Although these plays were inspired by real people and events, they should not be taken as factual accounts.

So how does one respect historical boundaries in the art of entertaining?

I like to move away from the close-up of that iconic individual to a panorama of their societal impact. And so, rather than re-inventing the biographical truth of Dr. King, my voice-guided approach is to focus on his followers. These three short plays, in their contemporary framework, do not physically feature the man himself. They are purposed to show how we, the bequeathed, are doing without him.

As you read these plays, I encourage you to make connections between your own life and the lives of the characters you are encountering. May the overall experience help you to imagine history in a fresh way and examine it as a tool that paves the way for personal growth. May this collection fuel your dreams of becoming a creative voice in this world.

BOUND BY BLOOD

"An individual has not started living until he can rise above the narrow confines of his individualistic concerns to the broader concerns of all humanity."

—MLK

CHARACTERS

JACQUELINE (JACKIE) SMITH: 20s. African American. A tenant and housekeeper at the Lorraine.

THEATRICE BAILEY: 40s. African American. The motel owner's brother.

The setting is the Lorraine Motel (Memphis, Tennessee), the night Dr. Martin Luther King Jr. was assassinated: April 4, 1968. It is immediately after Theatrice Bailey finished cleaning the blood from the balcony.

> *At rise, a room on the first floor of the Lorraine Motel on the night of Dr. Martin Luther King's assassination.*
>
> *Lights up,* JACKIE, *a housekeeper and resident of the motel is buttoning her uniform. There's a knock on the door. It's* THEATRICE. *Jackie hesitates.*

JACKIE. Who's there?

THEATRICE *(offstage)*. Theatrice Bailey. Walter's brother. He wanted me to check on you.

JACKIE. I'm okay, Theatrice.

THEATRICE *(offstage)*. Can I see for myself?

JACKIE hesitantly opens the door.

THEATRICE. I was just checkin' on all the residents since Walter had to leave.

JACKIE. If that's his way of seein' if I still plan on workin' my shift, then tell him yeah, I can work.

THEATRICE. Been one hell of a night. Be sure and clock in. Stay off the third floor.

He starts to leave.

JACKIE. I saw you up on the balcony . . . You get it all up?

THEATRICE. Ain't ever gone be all up.

JACKIE. You see Reverend Abernathy and Reverend Jackson—

THEATRICE. Yeah, I seen they asses.

JACKIE. They cry? Ain't seen too many men cry.

THEATRICE. It was somethin'—wanna see somethin'?

JACKIE. What . . .

He steps outside and returns to the threshold, holding a jar with blood in it.

JACKIE. What is it—

THEATRICE. Ain't no tomato paste.

*He sets the jar back outside and looks around
before returning to the room.*

THEATRICE. Sure is quiet out there. Ain't it strange how
quiet it's done got?

JACKIE. Everybody just stunned. Bea told me 'bout your
sister-in-law.

THEATRICE. Yeah. She alright . . . for now. Walter said she
just stroked out.

JACKIE. A stroke?

THEATRICE. Peculiar. Tonight's just—

JACKIE. When you talk to Walter tell him I'm praying for
Loree.

THEATRICE. Pray for us all. Pray for the blood that man
had to shed and me for sweepin' up the shit.
Excuse my mouth.

JACKIE. You alright . . . you was sweepin', too, out there
. . . Dr. King said one time . . . let me get it right
. . . "if a man is called to be nothin' but a . . . street
sweeper . . . then he should sweep streets like
Michelangelo painted, like Beethoven wrote music
or like . . . Shakespeare wrote . . . poetry . . . He
should sweep 'em so good that all the folks say—
here lived a great man who did his job well."

THEATRICE. Yeah well, I was a street sweeper today. You
should've—no—you couldn't've . . . the blood was
so . . . the smell was so . . .

*He pulls his handkerchief out and begins to
cough into it. JACKIE, sickened by the night's*

3

events, darts into the restroom. She coughs,
gags.

THEATRICE. I'm sorry, Jackie . . . *(Holding back his cough.)*
You alright . . . I ain't mean to . . . I just ain't never
had to clean up no river of blood before . . . You
got any soda—I'll get you a soda . . .

He gets two sodas out of the icebox.

THEATRICE. Picture man gone be rich one day. Been
'round here all day snappin' that camera. I mean
the man is snappin' everything—King's room, his
car, even takin' pictures of the building across the
street.

JACKIE *(offstage).* God forbid I ever see any pictures from
this night. Coward bastard—across the street. I
heard the shot!

THEATRICE. I heard it, too! One day them photographs
gone be worth a lot of money, you watch what I
tell ya . . . He even got a picture of me . . . sweepin'
the blood off the balcony . . .

JACKIE comes out of the restroom.

JACKIE. He did?

THEATRICE. Sho did . . . Best be gettin' back to work.

JACKIE. How does Walter expect us to work, huh?

THEATRICE. *(Handing her a soda.)* Oughtta settle your
stomach.

JACKIE. How he expect us to work.

THEATRICE also has a soda.

4

THEATRICE. Somebody's always gotta work. You think I wanted to clean up all that blood. Hell no. But somebody had to do it. All these folks runnin' around here—smart folks, mind you—and it ain't occurred to nobody that the blood gotta go. Everybody just steppin' over the blood. All on the balcony. Steppin' over the blood—ain't nobody stopped to think, "Okay, now, who's gone clean the blood up." I sat back long as I could then I was like, "Give me the damn broom." All these important folks—reverends, doctors, lawyers—

JACKIE. Ain't wanna mess up them suits.

THEATRICE. If Mayor Loeb go down right now, you better believe somebody got a job to do.

JACKIE. He need to go down. He's the one who should've gone down. Talkin' bout this ain't New York and the sanitation workers ain't gone gain nothin' by ignoring the law. Maybe Memphis need to be more like New York. Yeah. Maybe he need to go down . . . buildin' across the street, huh?

THEATRICE. Reckon if I had me a camera I'll be takin' pictures too.

JACKIE. I think it's a shame. Takin' pictures—he ought to be ashamed.

THEATRICE. He alright. He just snappin' and gettin' out the way.

JACKIE. It's just too much. Folks ain't wanna respect his flesh, least they can do is respect his blood. Let him rest in peace and let us mourn—and why you do that, huh? Why you got that man's blood in that Mason jar?

THEATRICE. Hell, I don't know.

JACKIE. You ain't got no respect neither.

THEATRICE. I respect the King.

JACKIE. Then why you do that? It ain't even sanitary and you work in housekeepin'. You know that ain't sanitary.

THEATRICE. Just seem like it'll be worth somethin' one day.

JACKIE. You ain't no better than the picture man.

THEATRICE. I have a dream.

JACKIE. Who you supposed to be—

THEATRICE. I have a dream today—

JACKIE. I'm clockin' in—

THEATRICE. That one day. A man named Theatrice Bailey will be famously known as the brother who swept the blood of Dr. Martin Luther King Jr. A man who preserved the blood of his leader in a Mason jar he washed jelly out of in the break room of the Lorraine Motel. I have a dream today. That a young housekeeper by the name of Jacqueline Smith who ain't got a pot to piss in or a window of her own to throw it out of—

JACKIE. Man, don't be callin' me out—

THEATRICE. —will one day be known as the woman whose room was below the balcony. Who was off yesterday, but would have delivered the King's

6

towels if they didn't take him down. That a couple of nobodies who just worked in housekeeping and maintenance, who ain't never owned anything but a struggle, will be able to tell white folks you gotta pay to hear my side of the story. I got a dream today—

JACKIE. I'm clockin' in.

THEATRICE. That the ghetto out there. The slums out there that rent for a hundred and fifty a month will one day be replaced by condominiums that rent for one thousand five hundred. And every doctor and every lawyer and every restaurant will want a piece of this neighborhood—shit—yeah, I got a dream.

JACKIE. Let me tell you somethin', Theatrice Bailey. Our leader. Our Jesus. Is gone.

THEATRICE. Come on now, Jackie. He wasn't no Jesus.

JACKIE. Why not, man? He died for us, didn't he? In his own way he died for you and me.

THEATRICE. He was a man. A damn good man. And you better believe they gone capitalize on that good man. The way I see it, this man done got shot on the balcony of this hotel. This white boy been taking pictures for damn near ten hours. We are standing on the foundation for a future historical landmark. I can just see thousands of dollars— millions of dollars—goin' into this place. Hell, they should just leave everything like it is and start buildin' a museum tomorrow. Walter ain't no fool, you know.

JACKIE. Just like a nigger. You even dream like a white man. You make me sick.

JACKIE goes back to the restroom.

THEATRICE. I'm just seeing the big picture. There's a big picture here. After tonight, you really think they're gone keep on rentin' rooms here? Who gone wanna stay here?

JACKIE. *(Returning to the room.)* I live here.

THEATRICE. You won't when folks are payin' forty and fifty dollars to come see where the King got took down. Just watch. Question is, who are the white people that's gone make it happen.

JACKIE. You and Walter are truly cut from the same cloth. All you think about is money. You think Martin Luther King really wants a million-dollar museum built in his honor? You think that's what Coretta Scott wants?

THEATRICE. Hell yeah.

JACKIE. The man died fightin' for garbage men. Garbage men. And folks like me who can't afford no god-damn forty-dollar museum ticket.

THEATRICE. Don't he deserve it?

A beat.

THEATRICE. He deserve it, don't he.

JACKIE. He wouldn't let 'em evict us. He wouldn't . . . He wouldn't let 'em do it . . .

A beat.

THEATRICE. I'm sorry. I was just . . . we gotta learn to see
the big picture sometimes. That's all . . . Come
here.

    She refuses his embrace.

THEATRICE. I'm tryin' to love on you. Dr. King want me
to love on you.

JACKIE. Wash your hands first . . . You scooped up blood,
man.

THEATRICE. That's Martin Luther King's blood. Ain't
nothin' wrong with that blood—

JACKIE. Just wash your hands.

    He goes into the restroom, washes his hands,
    and returns wiping them on his pants. She lets
    him hug her. Their embrace is more awkward
    than genuine. She pulls away.

JACKIE. I don't usually hug on folks . . . I'm alright now.

THEATRICE. You sure was upset. I probably went too far.
Sorry 'bout that.

JACKIE. Sorry for calling you out your name. You ain't
no nigger.

THEATRICE. Sure as hell ain't. The word is Negro, says
Dr. King.

    Police sirens.

THEATRICE. Even they still got work to do.

JACKIE. Hm.

The sirens intensify.

THEATRICE. Come on, I'll walk you out. Be sure and clock in. Keep away from the third floor. It's too much . . .

THEATRICE opens the door and JACKIE freezes.

THEATRICE. Jackie?

She can't move.

THEATRICE. Take the night off.

Silence. Finally, she nods.

THEATRICE. "Walk 'em easy 'round de heaven . . ."

He picks up the jar containing the blood of Dr. Martin Luther King Jr.

JACKIE. Could you leave it?

THEATRICE looks at her.

JACKIE. I know it sounds crazy—

THEATRICE. Naw. Naw. You ain't crazy.

THEATRICE sets the jar down. He touches JACKIE before walking away—again, it's more awkward than genuine. Once JACKIE is left alone, she touches the jar and the sirens hush. There's a slow fade to black and Jackie's hand and the jar of blood remain illuminated. She slowly lifts the jar, which now seems to glow in the palm of her hand.

End of play.

#COMMUNICATE

*"We must rapidly begin the shift from a
'thing-oriented' society to a 'person-oriented'
society . . ."*

—MLK

CHARACTERS

@MSRIGHT: A girl on-line of a popular social network such
as Facebook or Twitter.
@HISSIDE: An associate who often visits her page.

It's Martin Luther King Jr. Day in the digital revolution. The
dialogue may appear as projected text on the "screen of a
technical device". The dialogue can also be complemented
by voiceovers or the actors may be present on stage.

> *Lights up, a projected social media network.*
> *Images of Martin Luther King Jr. permeate the*
> *newsfeed. We then see images of President*
> *Barack Obama and Dr. King together—images*
> *and literature that suggest Obama is King's*
> *dream being fulfilled. We then see a moving*
> *cursor on the electronic device. A profile page*
> *belonging to @MSRIGHT is displayed. The infor-*
> *mation on her page may suggest certain charac-*
> *teristics and details of her life such as a*

"single" status or a definitive quote.
@MSRIGHT updates her status:

@MSRIGHT. I dnt understand why people are celebratin #MLK. Whats to be honored bout a man who cheated on his wife? SMH #infidelity

@HISSIDE. @MSRIGHT: damn, you mad?

@MSRIGHT. @HISSIDE: Just sayin. You know he was wrong.

@HISSIDE. @MSRIGHT: were you there tho? how you know he cheated?

@MSRIGHT. @HISSIDE: I knew you'd be the first comment. #instigators SMH

@HISSIDE. @MSRIGHT: not instigatin just sayin. i thought a spouse determines what happens in a relationship . . .

@MSRIGHT. @HISSIDE: What are you talkin bout? The man was spose to be a christian and he cheated on his wife. #infidelity

@HISSIDE. @MSRIGHT: come on now get off #MLK. none of us are perfect

@MSRIGHT. @HISSIDE: I'm not sayin he should've been perfect.

@HISSIDE. @MSRIGHT: what then

@MSRIGHT. @HISSIDE: if some1 can waiver in their marital vows then a crucial component of their character is compromised #infidelity

@HISSIDE. @MSRIGHT: well whether or not someone in politics has fidelity issues has nothin to do with how effective / ineffective they are as a political leader

@MSRIGHT. @HISSIDE: OMG Fidelity has EVERY-THING to do with leadership! #endofconversation

@HISSIDE. @MSRIGHT: I guess

A beat.

@HISSIDE. @MSRIGHT: the civil rights movement was not affected by #MLK's affair.

@MSRIGHT. @HISSIDE: Right. You have a blessed day! #agreetodisagree

@HISSIDE. @MSRIGHT: with all due respect, this is why I avoid your type. #phonychristians

@MSRIGHT. @HISSIDE: Then why are you always on my page?

@HISSIDE. @MSRIGHT: cuz u cute

@MSRIGHT. @HISSIDE: lol Thank you.

@HISSIDE. @MSRIGHT: Lunch?

@MSRIGHT. @HISSIDE: I thought you usually avoid my type.

@HISSIDE. @MSRIGHT: #exception

@MSRIGHT. @HISSIDE: #workin

@HISSIDE. @MSRIGHT: #MLK day

@MSRIGHT. @HISSIDE: I know, but I'm getting a lot done.

@HISSIDE. @MSRIGHT: on here?!?!?!?!?!

@MSRIGHT. @HISSIDE: lmao

@HISSIDE. @MSRIGHT: check my mailbox while u there

@MSRIGHT. @HISSIDE: Already did. You have nothing. #imalilnosey

@HISSIDE. @MSRIGHT: K

A beat.

@HISSIDE. @MSRIGHT: how about we have dinner and finish this #MLK convo? i think you do have some valid poi

There's a pause. HISSIDE *deletes the current message and types:*

@HISSIDE. @MSRIGHT: don't work too hard.

@MSRIGHT. @HISSIDE: K

@HISSIDE. @MSRIGHT: TTYL.

@MSRIGHT. @HISSIDE: ;)

MSRIGHT *then clicks on one of* HISSIDE'*s albums and peruses photos of him. As the lights fade, the following quote by Dr. Martin Luther King Jr., appears in a newsfeed format:*

"We must rapidly begin the shift from a 'thing-oriented' society to a 'person-oriented' society. When machines and computers, profit motives and property rights are considered more important than people, the giant triplets of racism, materialism, and militarism are incapable of being conquered."

Blackout.

End of play.

PARADOX IN THE PARISH

"At the center of non-violence stands the principle of love."

—MLK

CHARACTERS

IVAN POWELL: Black male; early 30s; lawyer.
KYLA POWELL: Black female; early 30s; ex-lawyer
HOSTESS: White female; late 20s–mid 30s.
NIKKI: Mixed, "exotic-looking" female; 22; attractive with lots of energy.

The setting is a steakhouse in Baton Rouge, Louisiana, September 21, 2007.

> *At rise, an unusual Friday night in Baton Rouge, Louisiana. A day's gone by since the civil rights protest in Jena, Louisiana; and just a few hours previously Mychael Bell, one of the "Jena 6" teens, was denied bail.*
>
> *Lights up on* IVAN *and* KYLA POWELL, *sitting on a bench in the waiting area of a restaurant. It's been a long week. They have been waiting to be seated for ten minutes now and are both engaged in separate phone conversations on*

their cell phones. The HOSTESS *is seen behind a podium.*

IVAN.

And with that approach, Charles, the

children from her first marriage will

receive ownership of her community

property and all other assets for that

matter . . . I'm not in the proper place

to give my opinion on that . . . tell you

what just leave the affidavit on my

desk; I'll take a look at it in the do.

morning . . . all right, man.

KYLA.

But what throws me for a loop is

how so many blacks have gone

to a tiny Louisiana town to protest

and march, but when gang bangers

start shooting up their neighborhoods

nobody claims to see anything . . . girl,

we are something . . . but I love us . . . I

All right, girl, y'all be safe coming

back. Okay. Bye, girl.

He ends his call. She ends her call.

KYLA *picks up the newspaper and starts reading. The* HOSTESS *appears.*

HOSTESS. Isaac, party of two. Isaac, party of two, your table is ready.

IVAN. Did she think I said Isaac instead of Ivan?

KYLA. You said Ivan pretty clearly, babe.

16

He checks his watch and then subtly speaks to the white couple sitting across from them. It is not necessary that the audience sees the white couple.

IVAN. Anything interesting?

KYLA. It's all interesting.

IVAN. What's most interesting?

KYLA. Just some hate crimes. Prejudice. Little black boys going to jail. Take your pick. *(To that white couple.)* Hello.

HOSTESS. McCoy party of two. Your table is ready.

Assumedly, the white couple, sitting across from them, gets up.

KYLA. 'Bout time. White folks been lookin' at us crazy since we sat down.

IVAN. Kyla.

KYLA. What? *(A short beat.)* Okay. W folks.

IVAN. They've been looking at us crazy because you've been talking crazy.

KYLA. Who?

IVAN. You. All night you've been talkin' crazy—

KYLA. I think we both can agree it's been a crazy day.

IVAN. You're always talking crazy—

KYLA. You know, we've been married a whole year now, Ivan. You should know I'm not one to put on any fronts. I'm a still tell it like it is—

IVAN. I know, Kyla. I know.

17

KYLA. I know you know.

She continues reading the newspaper.

IVAN. How about a movie, huh?

She shrugs.

IVAN. What's showing? . . .

KYLA then flips to the Entertainment section and reads . . .

KYLA. *Daddy Day Camp, Rush Hour 3, The Invasion, Resurrecting the Champ—*

IVAN. *Resurrecting the Champ,* what's that about?

KYLA. *(Reading)* "Up-and-coming sports reporter rescues a homeless man only to discover that he is, in fact, a boxing legend believed to have passed away."

IVAN. Heard about that movie. Who's in it?

KYLA. Samuel L. Jackson.

IVAN. Ah, that's my boy.

KYLA. Well, guess what. Your boy is playing the homeless guy.

IVAN. So?

KYLA. So it sounds to me like another . . . W writer's attempt at writing about us.

IVAN. Well . . .

KYLA. What?

IVAN. We're not even writing about us.

KYLA. *What?*

IVAN. And what we do write has no depth.

KYLA. We're not writing our movies the way *they* want us to write our movies.

IVAN. What else'd you say was showing—*Rush Hour 3*— Chris Tucker, right?

KYLA. Right.

IVAN. Wanna check that out?

KYLA. Sure. Let's go see the white detective's black sidekick.

IVAN. Jackie Chan is . . . never mind.

KYLA. Capitalizing on stereotypes. Now that's deep writing. Oh, Cuba Gooding Jr. is in this *Daddy Day Camp* movie. It's not *Boys in the Hood,* but hey, you wanna go see Cuba—

IVAN. No. Let's just eat and go home.

Silence.

KYLA. How about bowling.

IVAN. Nah. Red Sox are playin' tonight anyway. Wonder if there's any room at the bar? . . . Think she might've forgot about us?

KYLA. How can she forget about us, Ivan?

IVAN. It's not even that busy—

IVAN gets up and walks over to the HOSTESS's station.

IVAN. Excuse me, miss, we've been here a while and I was just seeing how long—

HOSTESS. Name?

IVAN. Powell . . .

HOSTESS. Ivan Powell, Esquire.

IVAN. Yes.

HOSTESS. Yeah, it'll be about twenty more minutes.

IVAN. You said that when you took my name fifteen minutes ago.

HOSTESS. Gattis, Lumpkin, and then Powell.

IVAN. Is there any room in the bar by any chance—

HOSTESS. The bar's full, Mr. Powell. Sorry. Excuse me.

> *She takes a couple of menus and walks off.* IVAN *walks back toward the bench with a smile.* KYLA *looks at him. He sits and puts his arm around her, lovingly.*

IVAN. Twenty minutes.

> KYLA *wants to say something, but exhales instead. She and* IVAN *both look at the newspaper.* IVAN *then speaks to another unseen, presumably white couple, now sitting across from them.*

IVAN. Hello . . .

> KYLA *then starts humming enthusiastically, Sly and the Family Stone's song, "Don't Call Me Nigger, Whitey." Ivan recognizes the song and gives her a critical look.*

KYLA. I'm playing, Ivan; dang, loosen your tie a little.

She folds the newspaper up. He takes it away from her.

IVAN. Have you checked the classifieds today?

KYLA. Yep . . .

IVAN. You see anything? . . .

KYLA. I saw some things . . .

IVAN. Anything worth pursuing? . . .

KYLA. Well, I've got another interview tomorrow.

IVAN. Oh yeah? Is it that new graphic-design company you were looking into—

KYLA. No. I talked to the owner over the phone and we just . . . we didn't vibe, you know what I mean?

IVAN. Okay . . .

KYLA. I'm interviewing with the bookstore downtown?

IVAN. Borders?

KYLA. Umoja Bookstore . . . remember we went in there two weeks ago. I bought some incense—

IVAN. Oh, *yeah.*

KYLA. What's up with that look?

IVAN. Just . . . good luck.

KYLA. Sure could use it. I'm a bit rusty, you know.

IVAN. You've got that job. It's your element.

KYLA. My element?

IVAN. Your element. Courtroom, my element. African bookstore . . .

KYLA. Oh. Okay. Love you.

IVAN. Love you, too.

Silence. KYLA *takes the newspaper back and rereads an article.* IVAN *checks his watch.*

KYLA. Mm. Every time I read it, it gives me chills.

KYLA. What?

KYLA. Sixty thousand protesting in Jena, Louisiana, and no violence. Martin Luther King would've been proud, huh? You know Janelle, my beautician. I just got off the phone with her and said she went with her church. She said it was so powerful. Shook Jesse Jackson's hand and everything. Can you believe that?

IVAN. Did she see Sharpton?

KYLA. Mm hm.

IVAN. *(Chuckling)* He let her do his hair?

KYLA *doesn't laugh.*

KYLA. We should've marched, Ivan. We should've gone to support those boys—

IVAN. You had an interview, Kyla. And I'm trying to make partner.

KYLA. What are you saying now—

IVAN. I'm saying keep your eyes on the prize.

KYLA. You know how I feel about that film. Listen to what this fool said, *(Reading)* "I wish these people marching and screaming 'Free the Jena Six' would get a grip and think for themselves. The six on one

22

beating had nothing to do with the hanging of the three nooses. It was a separate incident. People need to think for themselves and find out the facts, not the fantasy."

IVAN. The guy's entitled to an opinion. It's not a bad opinion.

KYLA. Whatever. You know these . . . "Ws" don't understand.

IVAN. I think they do. This thing affects that entire community.

KYLA. It affects *us*.

IVAN. Can I see that? *(She hands him the newspaper, and he tosses it.)* They've got pretty good steak here, don't they . . .

KYLA. We're a hundred and fifty miles from Jena, and we're getting looked at all kind of ways. I'm telling you, Ivan. We still have a long way to go in this country as far as race relations are concerned.

IVAN. Kyla. Baby. It's Friday. I'm not tryin' to play Malcolm X and Betty Shabazz tonight. I'm chillin'.

KYLA. I'm sorry, Ivan. I know you had a long day. Why don't you tell me about your day? How was your day?

IVAN. Pretty damn good.

KYLA. How so?

IVAN. Productive meetings with clients. A nice chef's salad at lunch.

KYLA. Ivan.

23

IVAN. What?

KYLA. Tell me.

IVAN. Tell you what?

KYLA. About your clients. About your cases.

IVAN. Why?

KYLA. Because I'm interested.

IVAN. Because you miss being a lawyer.

KYLA. I don't miss being a lawyer, you know what . . .
Forget it.

IVAN. What?

KYLA. *Why am I still interested?*

IVAN. Most lawyers land well on their feet after taking
time off.

KYLA. This is not a hiatus, Ivan . . . am I ever going to
find my niche?

IVAN. It's only been few weeks.

KYLA. It's been a month. I've been unemployed for a
month and . . . I haven't found my niche. I thought
I could tap into my creative side, but I can't seem
to stop analyzing everything . . . What if I open
my own business?

IVAN. You must've skipped "The Economic Decline in
America" in world news.

KYLA. Forget it.

> *IVAN checks his watch.*

IVAN. I could eat a whole chicken—feathers and all . . .
What kind of business, Kyla?

KYLA. This may seem a little outside of my character, but
. . . you know how much fun I had planning our
wedding?

*IVAN's cell phone rings. He looks at it and
silences it.*

IVAN. Go ahead.

KYLA. Like the article, with today's economy, no one
wants to invest twenty thousand dollars into a
wedding. We didn't. And everybody's still talking
about how elegant our ceremony and reception
was. If they only knew I did it all under ten grand.

IVAN. Hm.

KYLA. Moderate Matrimony, Incorporated . . . Brides on
a Budget, Incorporated?

IVAN. A wedding planner?

HOSTESS. Gattis, party of four.

KYLA. I was thinking about starting off as a part-time
consultant. You know, build my street credibility
and then, yeah, a full-time wedding planner . . . so?

IVAN. I'm sorry, Kyla. I really can't think like I want to
right now. Can I eat, get my levels right, then talk
about this?

KYLA. Sure . . . Love you.

IVAN. Love you, too . . .

KYLA. Ivan?

IVAN. Hm?

KYLA. I think that girl at the bar is waving at you.

IVAN looks.

IVAN. Oh. *(Waving.)* What's up, Nik.

KYLA. Nik?

IVAN. Chrystal's sister, Nikki.

KYLA. Oh. She doesn't look like Chrystal.

We see NIKKI.

NIKKI. Ivan.

IVAN. How you doing, girl?

NIKKI. I'm good. We called you.

IVAN. Shoot, I thought Chrystal was calling me about some work. I'm done.

He waves to Chrystal, whom we don't necessarily see.

NIKKI. We've been watching y'all for like five minutes. I wanted to tell you that I put in an application for that administrative specialist position at the firm.

IVAN. Man, if you land that you'll be working for Cartwright, himself.

NIKKI. Yeah. I'm so nervous.

IVAN. Nervous for you. It'll be a nice little in to the firm while you go to law school. Hope you get an interview. Let me know if I can do anything for you.

NIKKI. Do you really think it's a good place for me, Ivan?

IVAN. Sure! You belong in a law firm. It's your element.

NIKKI. Thanks.

IVAN. What you know about dark liquor?

NIKKI. Please. I'm twenty-two.

IVAN. Have you met Kyla? This is my wife, Kyla.

NIKKI. Nice to finally meet you.

KYLA. Likewise. So, you're Crystal's little sister.

NIKKI. I am.

KYLA. I didn't even know Crystal had a sister.

NIKKI. I'm surprised as much as I come by the office buggin' her and Ivan.

IVAN. You don't bug us. She doesn't bug us.

NIKKI. I was gonna come by today, but—man, are y'all keeping up with the news? It's like a bunch of racism going on in Jena.

IVAN. We're aware.

NIKKI. I don't know why they won't turn the televisions to something else. About an hour ago, this black dude at the bar started chantin' "Free Jena Six. Free Jena Six." Manager called the police.

KYLA. What?

NIKKI. Mm hm. Officer made him leave, too. Said he was provoking violence.

KYLA. Bullshit.

NIKKI. "United we stand, divided we fall." That's how I see it.

IVAN. And I don't see race, color, or creed in that powerful statement.

27

NIKKI. Neither do I—uh oh, I can see the bottom of my glass.

IVAN. Tell Crystal she didn't have to come speak to me.

NIKKI. She tried to call you. I think she and the bartender might elope tonight though. They don't even know each other, and already, they're in love.

IVAN. It can happen.

HOSTESS. Lumpkin, party of five. Your table is ready.

NIKKI. Yeah. Well, you guys enjoy your dinner. Have a steak, Ivan. Lay off those salads for a chance.

IVAN. I will . . .

NIKKI walks off.

IVAN. . . . If we ever get a table . . . I didn't know she was gonna put in for that secretary job.

KYLA. Think they'll hire her?

IVAN. If minority's priority. Funny she mentioned that. I was actually thinking about picking up an application for you.

KYLA. An application for what?

IVAN. James Cartwright's administrative assistant.

IVAN gets up and asks the hostess for a menu. She slowly gives him one, and he returns to his seat.

IVAN. Let's go on and have our order ready.

KYLA. Why did you think that?

IVAN. Think what?

KYLA. That I'd want to be a secretary . . . for James Cartwright . . .

IVAN. I wasn't seriously thinking it . . . but it wouldn't be bad for you to get back in the legal element while working on your business plan. Might actually be therapeutic.

KYLA. Being a secretary? Being *his* secretary?

IVAN. We doing an appetizer—

KYLA. Working in a bookstore will be therapeutic, Ivan. Consulting brides—that'll be therapeutic—

IVAN. Be a wedding consultant. I'd rather you do that than come home everyday smelling like that incense.

KYLA. I happen to love that incense. It's calming. I also love the idea of working in a *black-owned business*. My family owns a newspaper, Ivan. They're black nationalists. I went to Xavier. I work better in a black environment—

IVAN. Exactly. You've been around black people all your life, Kyla. It's too easy. You've gotta get out of that element—how else are you gonna learn how to coexist—what better way to apply that old adage—without struggle there is no progress— how else are you gonna learn what it's like to endure?

KYLA. I know how to endure.

IVAN. Kyla, you gave up law. And let's not pretend the white partners who "never spoke to you" had nothing to do with it.

KYLA. We endured slavery, Ivan. Being black is a struggle.

IVAN. Okay, change the subject—

KYLA. And when people are hanging nooses in 2007, it's time to protest. This Mychael Bell . . . they've got him right where they want him.

IVAN. Kyla—I—okay . . . a black high-school student asks the principal whether blacks can sit under a tree that white kids gathered at every day. The principal told him yes—

KYLA. I know what happened, Ivan—

IVAN. Hear me out. Nooses were hung. That incident was followed by fighting. You said Martin Luther King would've been proud.

KYLA. I was talking about the march.

IVAN. Why were we marching?

KYLA. Because injustice anywhere is a threat to justice everywhere.

IVAN. A noose was hung. Fights broke out. What is there to be proud of? Really.

Silence.

KYLA. People can take the law into their own hands, Ivan. If they can do that, what's the use in law? What's the use in being a lawyer?

HOSTESS. Dunaway, party of two. Your table is ready.

KYLA. I thought we were next.

IVAN walks over to the HOSTESS's station.

IVAN. Miss, I think you may have uh, made an oversight. My wife and I were here long before that couple you just called.

HOSTESS. Name?

IVAN. Attorney Ivan Powell.

HOSTESS. My mistake. You're actually next.

IVAN. You're sure about this.

HOSTESS. Yes sir. Sorry about that.

IVAN. Thank you.

> *KYLA has approached the podium.*

KYLA. We want to be seated now.

HOSTESS. Your table isn't ready yet, ma'am.

KYLA. I know because you gave our table to the white couple that just walked in there—

IVAN. Kyla—

KYLA. Didn't you—

HOSTESS. Ma'am, please calm down and have a seat or I'll have to call my manager.

KYLA. I don't wanna talk to your manager.

IVAN. I apologize, ma'am. We'll wait.

KYLA. No, we won't. Seat us now.

> *Ivan pulls KYLA to the side.*

IVAN. What's the matter with you?

KYLA. We were just discriminated against.

IVAN. Lower your voice.

KYLA. Why? Because we made history in Jena, Louisiana, and now all the white people are mad? So mad they're gonna make us wait thirty minutes before they seat us in an empty restaurant? Are they even sitting colored folks at all tonight?

IVAN. This place is full of black people.

KYLA. Well, then, it must be us.

IVAN. Maybe it's you, Kyla.

KYLA. Whew. Must've felt good to get that off your chest. Feel better? I get that you're conservative, Ivan. I accept that. It's cute even. But what's it going to take for you to take a stand. I loved being a lawyer more than you did, but I took a stand. I gave it up so I could pull up to work with a smile on my face. It's called passion. Passion for your people.

IVAN. I'm doing what I have to do. No, I may not love practicing law, but I like it. And it takes care of us. I'm doing what I have to do.

KYLA. And I'm telling you that you shouldn't have to settle.

IVAN. I settled for a lot of things in my life . . .

HOSTESS. (Making a mark on her paper) Powell . . .

IVAN. And I don't mind making sacrifices that's what adults do.

IVAN prepares to follow the HOSTESS.

KYLA. Take me home.

IVAN. What?

32

KYLA. Take me home now.

IVAN. We ain't in high school—

KYLA. I know, you're an adult.

KYLA exits.

IVAN. I ain't never gonna eat.

HOSTESS. Are you people dining with us tonight, sir—

IVAN. No, we're . . . *you people?*

HOSTESS. We have other people to seat.

IVAN. No. Sorry.

*He quickly exits the restaurant to find KYLA
standing next to a valet parking sign.*

IVAN. Are they bringing the car around?

KYLA. Yes.

Silence.

IVAN. Still keep pizza coupons in your purse?

KYLA. I thought you wanted steak.

IVAN. I do.

KYLA. Why settle.

IVAN. Kyla, I didn't mean—

KYLA. I know the feeling. I settled for law, and I was
forced to make a radical decision.

IVAN. And I support you. I just have to get used to this
whole wedding planning career. It might take a
little time, but I'll get used to it.

KYLA. You don't get it.

IVAN. Not totally, but I respect it.

KYLA. What's going to happen when you make a radical decision just so you can say you truly love the woman you're married to . . .

IVAN. What?

KYLA. Just tell me what you settled for.

IVAN. How could you think I don't really—

KYLA. I wanna know.

IVAN. Alright . . . Maybe I settled when . . . I stayed here, in Louisiana . . . I've been here all my life and well . . . I wouldn't have mind practicing law somewhere else . . . in Atlanta or something—

KYLA. I knew it.

IVAN. Knew what?

KYLA. If you would've moved to Atlanta, you never would've met me at that Christmas party, and we wouldn't be married right now. By settling to stay here, you . . . you settled for me.

IVAN. That's *your* train of thought.

KYLA. Admit it. You want to be in Atlanta. You want to be married to someone like Nikki.

IVAN. Nikki?

KYLA. Aren't there plenty of Nikkis in Atlanta?

IVAN. Yeah.

KYLA. She's refreshing, isn't she? That's why you like talking to her. That's why you're a totally different person when you talk to her . . .

IVAN. Feel better?

A beat.

KYLA. It's just that we're so different. We're like branches on a tree growing in two totally different directions.

IVAN. But we share the same root, Kyla . . . you know you're the only one for me. Why are you acting like you don't know that?

KYLA. Because I don't.

IVAN. What's up with you? What happened to the confident woman I married?

KYLA. Unemployment.

A beat.

IVAN. Kyla, you are one of the most passionate human beings I know. You go for passion. That's something I wish I had enough courage to do. I wish I had that . . . so . . . I don't know, maybe we were both envious tonight. And I don't know about you, but that's an emotion I don't care to feel. I'd rather just love you for you. Because you are perfect for me.

KYLA. Even though I'm an orange.

IVAN. We're really not that different. We're both hard workers.

KYLA. We both believe in family.

IVAN. We both love to eat . . .

A beat.

35

KYLA. I'm fine with going back inside, Ivan. Really—

IVAN. I'm . . . not even feeling the vibe in there anymore . . .

KYLA. I love you.

IVAN. I love you more . . .

He holds her hand and it feels really good to her.

KYLA. Where the hell's the attendant with the car . . . be funny if he stole it or something.

IVAN. He wasn't a black guy, was he—

KYLA. Asian.

IVAN. —oh, good.

KYLA. Gay, too.

IVAN. Oh . . .

Blackout.

End of play.

By law, these plays cannot be produced without written or verbal consent from the author. For performance rights and a royalty quote, please contact:

> University of Arkansas
> Department of Drama
> Kimpel Hall 619
> Fayetteville, AR 72701
> 479-575-2953